SMOOTH OPERATOR

Richard Jarman
and the Advertising Archives

CONTENTS

Introduction 4

Introduction

We don't see his type so often now, but back then he was the ultimate male icon. He was charming. Dashing. Debonair. He was a lady's man. He was the sort of man who was very much at home on a bar stool and who seldom lit his own cigarette. And if he wasn't decanting himself a whisky into a crystal tumbler, he was practising his golf swing in a pair of beige slacks.

He was hot. He was hairy. He was probably wearing crimplene.

But women were wise to be wary of his sort: this male of species bit back. He was a ladykiller. He was the male version of a praying mantis or black widow spider. He was a gorgon in Cuban heels with a ramrod moustache. He was the quintessential alpha male. In the '70s, he wore a satin-effect smoking jacket and left Milk Tray on your bedside drawer. In the '80s, his bachelor pad was black and chrome, and he threw a red bedspread on his pull-down futon.

INTRODUCTION

Remember his type? As Sade would no doubt chime in: 'No need to ask. He's a smooth operator.' Yes, coast to coast, LA to Chicago, the smooth operator was the archetypal Western male. In the '60s, '70s and '80s, he was the image of masculinity for men (and women) to buy into, whether it was his aftershave, his chunky jewellery or his Y-fronts. For the first time in a long time, the male body was up for grabs.

My father appropriated an off-the-peg version of the smooth operator, albeit with a few twists of his own. He was more what you would term 'lathe operator' than 'smooth operator', but I remember one afternoon in 1978, when he drove into town in his tangerine-coloured hatchback and returned with a fuzzy perm and man-clogs. For the next few months, I watched him carefully tweak and tease his curls with an Afro comb, displaying the sort of dedication I would later see him give to pruning ornamental roses. And while his man-clogs gave him much needed height, they caused him to clatter around precariously, his exaggerated leg movements giving him the look of a wading duck, the curly perm on top completing the picture of Big Bird.

Dad also began spending an inordinate amount of time in the bathroom, coming out stinking of strange synthetic man-perfumes – unguent, powdered or liquid – smells that would have put many an effluent outlet pipe to shame. And he began unbuttoning his shirt low to reveal a sovereign medallion amongst sparse, but carefully cultivated, wisps of chest hair. I think it was about that time in his life that he started playing squash doubles and invested in a chest expander.

Dressed in a short dressing gown which he wore about the house and which showed more thigh than was perhaps appropriate, Dad would perform faux martial-arts displays to himself in the long mirror. Out went the nylon Y-fronts and in came the leopard-print tanga briefs, so when Dad did a high kung-fu kick, we were all well and truly 'tangared'. Not since Narcissus fell in love with the image of himself in the pool of Mount Helicon had a man seemed so enamoured with his own image.

 I was only nine years old at the time and too young to realise what was happening to him, but I knew that he wasn't normally a vain man: the baggy trunks and cut-off denim shorts that he wore almost non-stop during a holiday to Benidorm were testament to that. He wasn't, as we would say today, 'in touch with his feminine side' – he was very much a man's man and enjoyed doing manly things such as clearing the outside guttering and racing ferrets. Nor could it be said that he was much of dandy either; it was his brother Derek – and not my dad – who came

back from West Germany carrying a handbag, a fashion corker that's still spoken of to this day. Truth is, I merely assumed Dad was in the midst of a mid-life crisis and said nothing, preferring to leave him to have his mental breakdown in peace.

It's only now, nearly 30 years on, that I realise that my father was performing the most ancient of rites. He was paying homage to the masculine image. Put simply, he was preparing himself to go out on the pull. No longer with my mother, Dad was creating his own version of the male beautiful. With his new mane of hair, traditionally the symbol of male strength and virility, as well as the extra two or three inches afforded by his man-clogs, my father was hot to trot. Never mind 'Lock up your daughters', it was a case of 'Lock up your daughters *and* their Carmen heated rollers'.

However, the world into which my dad furtively dipped his man-clog wasn't the same as it had been when he and my mother had first gone a-courting in the late '50s. It had changed dramatically. In the '50s, the extent of male preening

involved nothing more than combing chip fat through your
hair and blowing the mothballs off your father's demob suit.
But by the late '70s, the female form was no longer the sole
focus of sexual desire. John Travolta was strutting his stuff in
Saturday Night Fever, and before you could say 'polyester
lounge suit', men the disco-dancing world over were squeez-
ing themselves into 12-inch bell bottoms and stuffing socks
down their groins.

The sexes had been in turmoil since the psychedelic '60s
melted the static gender roles of the '50s. Women were
being liberated through birth control and in the workplace.
By contrast, there were
the first mumblings that
men would soon
become surplus to
requirements, that
masculinity was heading
for crisis. The androgyny
of the '70s led us
nowhere fast and only
assisted in confusing the
mix, as men and women
looked for their lost iden-
tities in the approaching
'80s. Something was
happening on the high
street too. Off-the-peg
emporiums and mail-
order catalogues hit and
suddenly fashion
became affordable and

mass market – not the greatest omen in terms of quality it has to be said. However, I think we can blame the arrival of new man-made fibres and dyeing agents for the more experimental fashion crimes during this period.

It is through this period of flux that our hero, the smooth operator, boldly ploughed his furrow. Unabashed, he flew the flag for the male as sex god during a time of sexual uncertainty, and maybe that explains what's fascinating about him today. Dressed in the fashion shrapnel of the time,

the smooth operator stood for the age-old image of the sexually desirable male.

Men have preened and paraded themselves since they fell out of trees. In Western culture, the male image can be traced back to the *kouros* of Greek antiquity, later immortalised by Michelangelo's *David*. This Apollonian ideal – the broad shoulders, the expanded chest, the tight buttocks and the stiff pelvis – struts like a peacock aware of its admirers. All that's new in the pictures in this

book is that they're either doing this in the underpants section of a catalogue or they're modelling Gore-Tex.

There are, however, aspects of the smooth operator's character that both repel and intrigue us. If you set yourself up on a pedestal, you're asking to be knocked off – especially so if you're a man. For one, we suspect him of chauvinism. In the pictures that follow, if women aren't hanging off his neck, they're fingering his sunglasses or cooing at his crotch.

11

And while he may have been considered 'groovy' and 'with it' in his day, from our present-day perspective, he seems gloriously out of date.

He's vain too, and if there's one thing a woman admires less than a man who doesn't care about the way he looks, it's one who does. We don't like men to care (or be seen to care) about such surface-deep flimflam. Men are supposed to hunt, gather nuts and change carburettors in second-hand cars. Even today's so-called metrosexual man, with his skin-care products and plucked eyebrows, is essentially a figure of fun.

But I think there's something else deep beneath our stone-throwing. If a man loves his own reflection, we suspect it wouldn't take much for him to transfer that desire to another man's reflection. So that if the smooth operator is guilty of Narcissism, he might well enjoy another practice of the ancient Greeks, namely shirt-lifting. That, traditionally, has been a great way of bringing the macho heterosexual man down a peg or two. Such is the lot of the smooth operator. He walks a precarious tightrope between impressing the ladies and convincing them he really wouldn't be interested.

But I think the smooth operator has the last laugh on us. We think these hairy beasts of the sex-war jungle are antique relics, Neanderthals that have been selected out of existence by modern sensitive man. Maybe that's their comedy value, but I urge caution. It is merely his fashion – the man-drag – that has changed to fit in with modern norms. The ancient rules of sexual attraction haven't changed one iota. Like the *kouros*, my dad in his man-clogs or today's modern sensitive man, the smooth operator is merely a chapter in the history of men masquerading as men.

The smooth operator's dead. Long live the smooth operator.

Facial hair

Nowadays, facial hair is largely favoured by Middle Eastern dictators and gay bears in leather chaps, but back in the '70s, face fuzz was more popular than flock wallpaper and melon boats put together. Moustaches, beards and lamb-chop side-burns were cool, and men everywhere looked like Turkmenistani goatherds on the loose. If you didn't have the regulation bouffant mane with matching whiskers, you might as well have spent your evenings at night school doing car maintenance classes, because no woman would give you a second look.

Moustaches were hit and miss affairs as babe magnets: for

every wannabe Magnum P.I. and Robert Redford were a thousand Roland Rats. The best thing was to go for the ultimate Lion King look, which involved a lacquered hairdo, moustache and beard for that 360-degree hair experience: turn your head upside down and no one would notice the difference.

FACIAL HAIR

When curly perms and ramrod moustache combos came in at the fag end of the decade, every man looked like Bob Carolgees, the bloke who used to have Spit the Dog. Either that or they looked like Spit the Dog.

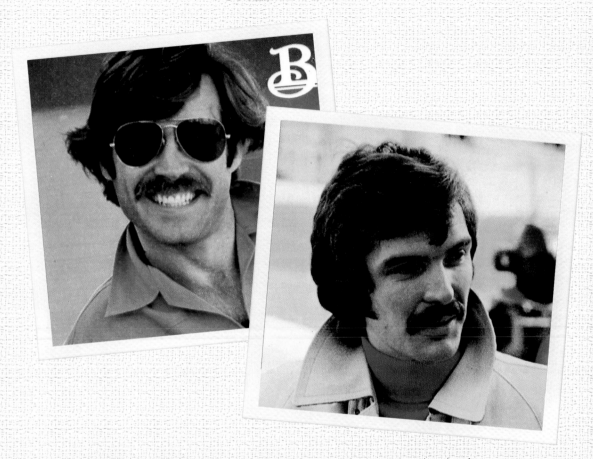

For the smooth operator, facial hair was akin to getting back
to nature and looking worldly wise – like Gandalf or Grizzly
Adams, say. For the woman, however, the experience
was more akin to being snogged by a Yorkshire terrier on
heat or by something that was last seen running for its life up
a drainpipe.

Body hair

Like the Wolf Man, body hair was the defining feature of the smooth operator. Or should we say hairy operator? Not for him hours spent shaving, plucking and waxing. The only time he came into contact with hot wax was when he slipped with his candle (free in an Old Spice Gift Box) in a blackout during the Three Day Week. Smooth operators showed off their bodies and let their hairs hang loose; this was the Age of Aquarius after all.

A date for a woman in the '70s was like meeting the ancestors or dining with a monkey. And, whereas modern man shares 98.4 per cent of his DNA with chimps, by contrast, the '70s smooth operator was genetically no different to his monkey cousins; the only difference being that a monkey had a touch better table manners.

BODY HAIR

Chest hair was a must, but if the smooth operator could grow the stuff that spread across his back and sprouted up at the collar, so much the better. And if you couldn't grow body hair, a chest wig would do – what's more, they doubled up as oven-scouring pads when you were done wearing them.

For most, body hair wasn't a problem, as these men were naturally hirsute; so hairy in fact that they could easily have been combed and shown for best of breed at Crufts. On the downside, however, they also attracted the first animal-to-human incident of fox-mange.

Sportswear

In the '70s, if your moustache and mullet were as fluffy as your terylene towel, you were a sportsman. Every dude broke out in a sweat. Mind you, even the smallest set of stairs was a bugger when you were on 60 a day. But, back then, smoking and sport were complementary activities. Squash, for example, was played with racket in one hand and a tab end in the other. Best sporting brands were those containing vouchers, so you could save up for a crystal decanter set or a three-speed drill.

SPORTSWEAR

By the '80s, the jogging craze hit, and male genitals were packed tight in trackie shorts. Freeze-dried vacuum packaging was put to shame. Canary-yellow Walkmans were all the rage too, and blokes lumbered around the parks to the sound of Sheila & B Devotion on full blast. How many were lost under the axle of an oncoming articulated lorry may never be known.

SPORTSWEAR

When package holidays made it to the Alps, smooth operators took to branded ski-wear in a big way, and the 'Eddy "The Eagle" Edwards' look was in: luminous jumpsuits, headbands, white sunblock for the lips and fluorescent sunblock for the nose. Older smoothies aspired to timeshares in Portugal and a round of golf. Looking like minor celebrity game-show hosts such as Jimmy Tarbuck or Lenny Bennett was in, as was anything in Gore-Tex.

Leatherwear

Nowadays only found in clubs under railway arches in the East End and in Vauxhall, once upon a time leather was the uniform for the strutting ladykiller. Alvin Stardust sang 'Ma Coo Ca Choo' wearing leather gloves and Mud danced to 'Tiger Feet' in leather trousers.

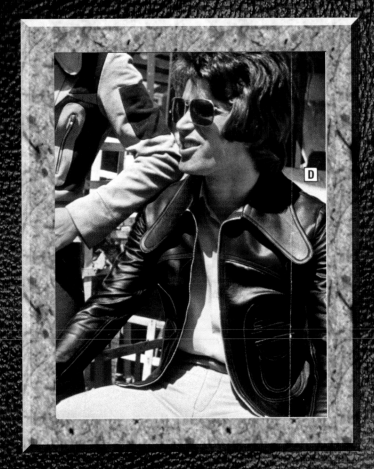

Leather trousers became really popular in the late '70s, after Hot Gossip appeared on the *Kenny Everett Video Show*, and every Casanova took to competitive disco dancing with a pint of Arctic Light in one hand and a fag in another.

LEATHERWEAR

Leather goods seemed fantastic back then; only now do we know where all those poor beasts ended up that fell to their deaths at the Grand National. There were many *el cheapo* imitations flogged down at the market in the '70s and '80s, too, often made of polyvinyl chloride – perfect for that 'World of Leather settee with matching pouf' look.

The other leather look was more biker in appearance, the jackets of which had tasselled arms and chest-hair-snagging zips, with leather boots for that complete greasy rock-minger look. Other variations on this theme were inspired by motor-cycle legend Barry 'Splash It All Over' Sheen and Formula One's James Hunt. And in his faux racing-driver leathers, many a smooth operator looked like a complete car crash.

Aftershave

If it was affordable and stank like cat's piss, chances were it found shelf space in a smooth operator's bathroom. Wearing aftershave was about being a man, and accusations that they were somehow poncy, perfumed or feminine were likely to land the accuser with a right hook.

Macho Musk Oil is mucho macho.

Every ninja with chest hair and a box-kit home perm drenched himself in these potions, the chemical properties of which would not have been out of place in a bottle of paint stripper or a pond in the more radioactive parts of the Ukraine. Usually administered after a shave with a disposable razor, the instructions on the bottle failed to advise the calling of an ambulance to take one to the nearest hospital's skin-burns unit.

AFTERSHAVE

With scents limited to musk or spice, the whiff was more likely to turn a woman's stomach than her head. These thick aromas were the calling card of the smooth operator, using the same principle as a dog cocking its leg up in a bus shelter; the only difference being that dog's piss smells nicer.

A bottle of Brut was shaped like one of those vinegar bottles they have down the chippy and promised to make you smell like Henry Cooper. A bottle of Tabac promised to make you smell like Peter Wyngarde, even if it was when he was smoking a packet of fags.

These potions had all the animal magnetism of a polecat. On the upside, however, they usefully doubled as applications to ward off mosquitoes and other forms of blood-sucking invertebrates.

Peter Wyngarde smells...

great.

The smell he puts on each morning is Tabac. Tabac Original After-shave. For the man of action.

TABAC ORIGINAL

Slacks

The embodiment of sensibleness yet informality, slacks brought the term 'loosely cut' to mail-order catalogue and golf club alike. Flat at the front, so the world could see which side he dressed, and square at the arse, slacks were pure woman magnets: they just couldn't get enough of them.

Slacks tended to come in colours such as grey, beige, camel and other variations on the theme dull. Otherwise, they were in Rupert Bear, 'Donald Where's Your Troosers', tartan in homage to the Bay City Rollers, lest we forget. Some slacks came in fun psychedelic patterns, a miscellany of trouser that, funnily enough, has yet to enjoy a return as a fashion trend.

SLACKS

Material-wise, we are talking nylon, poly nylon and anything that has a tendency to chafe your inside leg. When a smooth operator crossed his legs, the electric static generated was sufficient to stun a small mammal. With the stretch in the seat of the pants akin to that usually found on a trampoline or in a cord used for bungee-jumping, slacks proved incredibly versatile to the outdoors man, out on the prowl. Whether teeing off in the bunker or dragging his tartan caddy, the smooth operator and his slacks were ready for any hole in one.

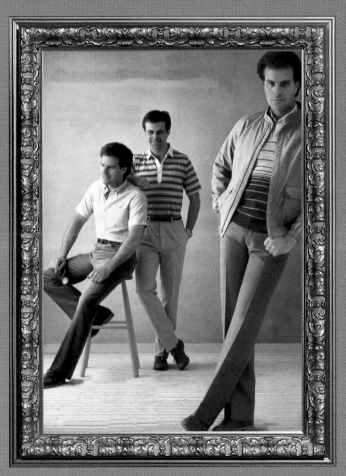

Slacks conjured up words such as 'relaxed' and 'languid', and that was the look that your common-or-garden slacks man meant to convey to the legion of ladies attracted to his nylon trousers. On the other hand, the word 'slack' also means inactivity and sluggishness, not the most alluring of images it has to be said.

Sunglasses

Now much preferred by the likes of Colonel Gaddafi and the more fashionable end of totalitarian despots, sunglasses had a tendency to spell 'wanker', especially so if a smooth operator was behind them. Smooth operators were best advised to avoid wearing sunglasses en masse as it made them look like cast members of *The Blues Brothers* or a branch division of the Romanian Secret Police.

Dynamic styles for men and women in lightweight Optyl™ frame material. ... See the world through Playboy Sunglasses ... the eyewear collection designed to fit your li...

The adverts for sunglasses at the time promised that if normal blokey wore them, he too would soon have a lovely lady put her hand down his vest or he'd be piloting a light aircraft. In reality, wearing sunglasses only afforded him the opportunity to look down random females' cleavages undetected. Mind you, they in turn could check their reflection for any lippy on their teeth so, overall, everyone was happy.

SUNGLASSES

Favoured by Erik Estrada from *CHiPS* as well as numerous drag queens on their day off, mirrored sunglasses became massive in the '70s. If everyone looked skyward at the same time they could have bounced back satellite signals to Sputnik or diverted a chartered aeroplane en route to Alicante.

In the '80s, skiing became mainstream and so much time was spent perfecting the wraparound-sunglasses look that too little time was spent actually learning to ski. But at least the smooth operator was assured that when he went arse over tit down a crevasse, he'd be doing so in branded shades.

Jewellery

A smooth operator liked his jewellery – particularly those chunky bracelets with his name engraved in italic writing or sovereign rings the size of meat dishes. However, the ultimate smooth-operator badge was the medallion.

JEWELLERY

The idea of the medallion was to make the smooth operator's chest hair a feature by drawing a woman's eyes to the bit between the open buttons. They also attracted magpies, which swooped from the skies to attack many a male chest for these shiny precious things, any plucked chest hair providing soft bedding back at the nest.

JEWELLERY

With all the aesthetic appeal of ornamental horse brasses, medallions were a smooth operator's disco bling. They swung around his neck like a lead weight or smashed into his teeth if he went jogging or ran for the bus. They also snagged his nipple hairs something rotten.

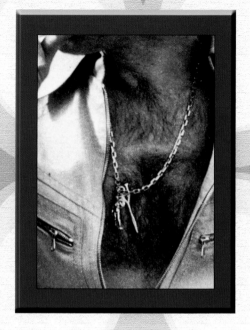

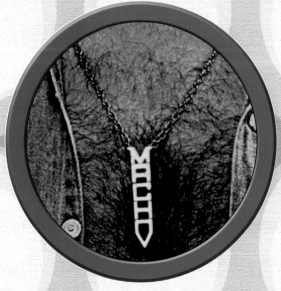

Medallions came in all styles. There was the standard medal size, which looked like chocolate money hanging off a Christmas tree, the medallions being only slightly more expensive but arguably still as tasteless.

And who can forget St Christopher, the patron saint of shit jewellery? Or the plastic shark's tooth, which promised ancient aphrodisiac qualities to the wearer but didn't deliver, on account of it being made of plastic. And then there was the golden nugget bar, truth if it were ever needed that all that glitters is not gold. It was probably won in fact on a penny-push machine in Blackpool. Other medallions were simply hand-me-down jewels hung from a gold chain. But what smooth operator didn't like showing off the family jewels?

Beachwear

When the Beach Boys made surfing and beachwear cool, smooth operators got their kits off and their skimpy trunks on. Beaches the world over – Rhyl, Pwheli and other exotic locations – were packed with more naked flesh than that seen during the elephant-seal mating season.

Special mention is needed for zip-up trunks, which proved very handy for emergencies, such as when being cut short and far from the nearest WC or when given the glad-eye by a stranger in the sand dunes. The downside of these bum-bags for the smooth operator was that he risked snagging his end in the zip on the way back in.

And what about the trunks with matching blouson beach combo, which came in sun-lounger and dining-room-curtain patterns?

Art

It's Jantzen's totally new look. A soft, stylish brief and shirt that stands you apart from any crowd. The set is of perfect-fitting Du Pont ANTRON nylon and LYCRA spandex. "Body Art." Wear it and watch all eyes follow you. Brief, $7.50 Shirt, $20.

For the promenade in the
'70s, shorts were big:
the type that were really
tight, with double stripes
and tiny slits at the side.
Or should we say smalls
rather than shorts? They
packed the smooth
operator in so tight he
could sustain a high-
octave note but couldn't
reproduce. Some shorts
made it into nightclubs
and proved useful for
skipping the double-dutch
and gyrating to
Imagination. In either
case, they proved more
effective in clearing the
dance floor than a
fire-alarm klaxon or the
first few bars of 'The
Birdie Song'.

These two busboys from
Club 54 in New York are
visiting their friend Audrey,
who's convalescing at a
Miami Gender
Reassignment Clinic.

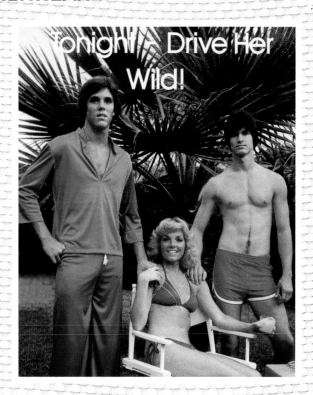

Tonight – Drive Her Wild!

Hair

Apart from snogging each other on the pitch, smooth-operator footballers enforced their male bonding through competitive hairdressing. Big hair equalled masculine strength, and it also allowed for a bit of cross-dressing too: Tarzan became Jane and Samson, Delilah – this was the beautiful game after all.

HAIR

The evil perm, as popularised by Chrissie Waddle and Glen Hoddle, was the high point in big man-hair. This came in two distinct types: the 'joke-shop curly' and the 'limp and shaggy'. The latter was favoured by footballers everywhere, who looked like Barbra Streisand in *The Way We Were*. Think Charlie George, Graeme Souness, Bryan Robson. However, the Lord of the Perm will forever be Kevin Keegan and his 'One Perm to Rule Them All.'

HAIR

Another smooth-operator calling card was wet-look hair. In the '60s and before, Brylcreem did the job and, with its revival in the '80s, the greasy-kid look was in. So too was wet-look gel. This made hair look wet but in fact set it rock solid until, that is, it rained, when it drained into the smoothie's eyes, burning them like acid.

In 1983, the curly perm and wet-look gel promised the 'Michael Jackson on the *Thriller* album cover' look. When smooth operators jumped in the sea with this lot lathered into their hair, the resulting slick necessitated the hosing down of sea birds with detergents for weeks.

Slick suits

The slick suit was the attire of the smooth operator out on the town and on the pull. Whether he was treating his lady-friend to chicken-in-a-basket at an Aberdeen Steak House, slipping her a Slow Comfortable Screw in a cocktail bar, or leading her by the hand to jive to 'Una Paloma Blanca', slick suits said snazzy. Natty. Dapper. Slick suits also said man-made material, maybe because they were made up of fibres that wouldn't have been out of place in an oil slick. Some of the suits looked like they were made from a material that had served as a pot of white emulsion in a previous life. However, the ultimate man-made fibre slick suit was the '70s' polyester lounge suit in safari khaki, suitable for going elephant-stalking in.

SLICK SUITS

Slick suits came in a cornucopia of colours; but there was, however, a propensity towards brown and, Lord have mercy, gingham. More Austin Powers than Austin Reed, slick suits read 'casual yet formal' and 'not too fussy yet smart'. They also read 'wine waiter' and 'pimp'.

Underwear

Before Nick Kamen showed his boxer shorts in the Levi's advert in 1985 and years before Mark Wahlberg held his crotch in a pair of white Calvin Klein's, men's underwear only came in two distinct types: briefs and Y-fronts.

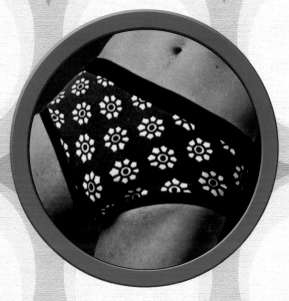

Briefs tended towards the more risqué end of the smooth-operator market and were small and bikini-bottomed in shape. Y-fronts, on the other hand, were for the man with a need for a larger undergarment, with an expansive acreage. In the vastness of these pants, the smooth operator could accommodate his cigarettes and his Gold Spot breath fresh-ener and still have room for his lunchtime sandwich box with matching thermos flask.

UNDERWEAR

Briefs said 'sexy beast', the adverts of the time showing men with pumas and other big cats straining on a leash. No doubt these suggested either he was concealing a big beast inside his panties or that he could bring a big pussy to heel by simply wearing them. Oh please!

UNDERWEAR

Y-fronts said 'practical' and provided a handy flap from which to enable the smooth pulling in and out of the vital organ. However, this didn't mean they couldn't be ladykillers too, coming in many bright colours, especially red, the colour we associate with love, lust and passion, as well as the shade of a baboon's backside when it's up for it. The problem with Y-fronts, and their matching vests and T-shirts, was that they led many a smooth operator to leave the house half-dressed to stand about in gangs on sand dunes looking cool.

Socks

Not all socks were the sort of grey depressing socks your grandad was buried in. The '70s' safari lounge suit demanded a hint of colour, and so even Wolsey, the traditional makers of socks, stretched to so-called 'Playsocks' so that men about town could know a sock in red, blue or green, and, if the advert on the right were to be believed, would be enabled to eat pastries in bed with four other naked men. They seem like fancy puffs – the cakes, that is. In the '80s, colours were out but white terylene broke out in bubonic proportions. What was once used for slamming a few squash balls about the court was now shown off between drainpipe trouser bottom and loafer.

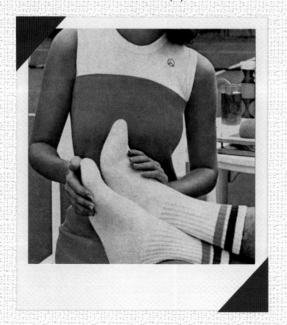

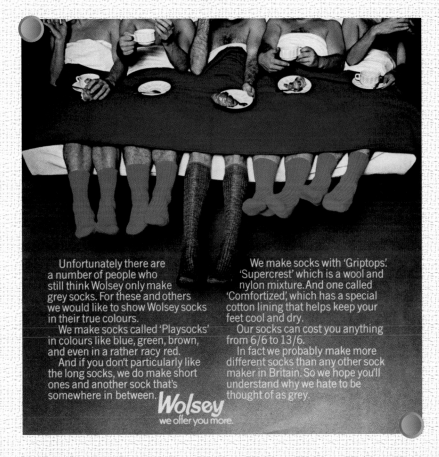

Unfortunately there are a number of people who still think Wolsey only make grey socks. For these and others we would like to show Wolsey socks in their true colours.

We make socks called 'Playsocks' in colours like blue, green, brown, and even in a rather racy red.

And if you don't particularly like the long socks, we do make short ones and another sock that's somewhere in between.

We make socks with 'Griptops'. 'Supercrest' which is a wool and nylon mixture. And one called 'Comfortized', which has a special cotton lining that helps keep your feet cool and dry.

Our socks can cost you anything from 6/6 to 13/6.

In fact we probably make more different socks than any other sock maker in Britain. So we hope you'll understand why we hate to be thought of as grey.

Wolsey
we offer you more.

Socks should be worn but not made into a feature. 'Never mix comedy and fashion,' it is commanded. So-called 'fun socks' also read, amongst other things, 'office prat', 'sad git', 'no mates', 'crap shag'. Smooth-operator fashion crimes here have included socks patterned with cartoon characters, slogans and small comedy penises.

Man at C&A
reinstate the Sunday best.

Just run a quiet check
over your week-end wardrobe.
Are you letting your weekday image down?
Resolve to relax in style.
Man at C&A have just assembled
a collection of Sunday bests de luxe
fit for the most civilised leisure living.
Highly respectable cloths,
finely styled and luxuriously finished.

Showing his gratitude (illustrated)
wearing his choice of our range in Terylene*/Worsted
with matching belt. £5.19.0.

Man at C&A

SOCKS

Another important sock rule is wear clean socks every day.
What we tend to forget now is how much everyone smelt
back then. In the '70s, if we weren't in drought, then the
public utilities were taking industrial action, with the result that
there was only enough hot water to wash about once a year.
When socks were worn over and over again, the sole became
as crunchy as the cheesy hard skin that collected inside.
Maybe this explains the smooth operator's obsession with
spraying on aftershave with a toxicity to rival Agent Orange.

Neckwear

Smooth operator tip: clever use of bright neckwear can play down an ugly face. It's the same principle as the medallion. The most cheerful of neckwear was the kipper tie, so-called because it was shaped like a kipper.

Kippers were patterned in loud stripes, paisley or any colour or pattern that could be guaranteed to clash with everything else. Often the kipper looked like someone had vomited over the smooth operator's shirt and, given the stench of the smooth operator's aftershave, such a reaction on a first encounter was not outside the realms of possibility.

NECKWEAR

The cravat, a strange neckerchief affair in patterns not dissimilar to Vimura wallpaper, gave the smooth operator that 'ever so slightly camp and fey' look that, in the androgynous '70s, drove the ladies wild. You see, the smooth operator wasn't ashamed of getting in touch with his feminine side (or anyone else's feminine side for that matter, especially a woman's), and this concession to dandyism was often combined with a satin-effect smoking jacket and a pair of slippers, to give that 'old cad cum chain smoker' image. It also gave him a look of a child molester in the Boy Scouts. No wonder it hasn't been adopted by successive generations of smooth operators.

NECKWEAR

Similarly, the dicky bow tie has enjoyed a mixed success revival-wise. The evening wear look is hard to get just right and, when combined with a coloured blouson shirt, can veer more towards Bernie Inn waiter than 007; the overall result made the smooth operator look more at home pulling a sweet trolley than pulling the ladies.

Knitwear

Woollens evoke a million autumnal mail-order catalogue pictures, all laughter and kicking through leaves. Looking like Noel Edmonds on *Multicoloured Swap Shop* was the aim, or perhaps a caribou herdsman from Greenland.

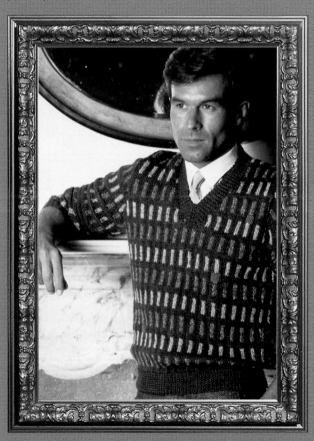

There was no end to the knitwear a smooth operator could choose from. There were turtlenecks or polo-necked sweaters, which, usually knitted too tight, made a feature of his man-breasts and provided him with the ultimate folk singer's look. There was the casual zipper cardigan, which could tastefully be worn over hairy chest and medallion but could necessitate the calling of the emergency services if unzipped with gay abandon.

And who can forget the sweater tunic, a sort of long hanging chunky cardigan with matching knitted belt for that quintessential peasant-from-the-middle-ages, men-in-tights look. In the '80s, smooth operators went for the patterned V-neck shaped sweater that came in Frank Bough diamond patterns.

All this knitwear gave the suggestion that the smooth operator was cuddly and teddy-bear-like and wanted to do nothing
more than get cosy, toasting his nuts by the fire. But it was
just another seduction ploy. No sooner had his lady friend
finished her snowball cocktail and Warnicks' chaser, than he
was down to his leopard-print Y-fronts … and then it really was
a case of jerkin off.

Workwear

The '80s have a lot to answer for: avocado-coloured bathroom suites, squirty cream and yuppies – as well as Kajagoogoo of course.

WORKWEAR

The '80s were about getting rich. The look of the decade involved big, big shoulder pads in jackets and long coats, to give every man that American footballer/Alexis Carrington look. Broad shoulders were a statement about the hubris of the decade. If the smooth operator turned his head too quickly, he'd knock himself out with his shoulder padding.

WORKWEAR

Suits were double-breasted with shiny veneers. Braces, too, enjoyed a revival, though on many a wannabe '80s smoothie, with his curly perm and moustache, he looked more like Bobby 'Rock on Tommy, You Got My Nipples' Ball than, say, a Wall Street yuppie.

Hair-wise, it was 'the bigger the hair, the bigger the packet'. Pay packet, that is. Somewhere between George Michael in the 'Careless Whisper' video and Princess Diana during the bulimia years: tongs, hairdryers and a family bucket's worth of mousse.

WORKWEAR

If he worked hard, he played hard too, and a hard smooth operator wasn't hard to find. When he took a lady-friend back to his bachelor pad for Chicken Kiev and Asti Spumante, it was like she'd died and gone to World of Leather heaven. Everything she sat on seemed to have been modelled on the interior of a fantasy sports car from one of his wet dreams. And everything, but everything, was in red, black and chrome.

Shirts

The shirt used to play merely a background role, providing an understated border to a colourful tie or a neutral background to a smart jacket. However, the smooth operator, with his chest hair, chunky jewellery and his mix and match, changed all that. He wanted to draw attention to his body, he wanted to say 'Look at the fine contours of my Apollonian physique' or, failing that, 'Look at the cascading roles of flab on my lager belly.'

'If you've got the body, we've got the shirt…' says the advert for the skintight shirt, but if you haven't, it should have continued, suck in your gut and hope for the best. And most smooth operators were nothing if not optimistic.

So the shirt became a fashion item in its own right. Shirts came in more fibres than you could shake a carpet warehouse at, and variations on the theme became 'male-blousons' or 'chemises'. Collars were big and open, coming in butterfly, triangle and highboy styles, opening up to reveal a bird's nest of chest hair with buttons undone as far down as the belly button. However, too much male stomach was too much for most women to stomach.

SHIRTS

On the good side, by dispensing with the need for a jacket, the smooth operator had one less layer of clothing to worry about before jumping into the sack. Also, he could get off on the feel of crimplene tickling his nipples.

Footwear

Having landed on the moon, in the '70s men realised how small and insignificant they were. Hence the fashion explosion in platform shoes. Short-arsed men everywhere experienced vertigo for the first time as well as the pleasure of a bird's-eye view of a woman's cleavage. Big feet were in, as was falling arse over tit if he had to walk more than two or three yards unaided.

FOOTWEAR

Usually worn with huge flapping flares, platforms gave a loud clack-clack-clack sound as the smooth operator lunged towards his victim across the dance floor. This resultant noise – about as quiet as a road digger – tended to drown out the sound of the disco hits of the time, such as Lena Martel. On the positive side, however, it alerted any unsuspecting female that a smooth operator was closing in on her.

FOOTWEAR

Colour-wise, different shades were à la mode and two-tone soft leather shoes with resin platforms were massive, literally, for a time. Polished so much that you could see up your own nose in them, two tones looked like something Coco the Clown would wear or something you'd go crown bowling in.

Clogs, curiously, also became trendy attire for men in the androgynous '70s. These were slip-ons with a heavy wooden sole and could usefully be deployed as wasp-swatters or for stunning any female should she not succumb to the smooth operator's advances.

The big '80s' shoes were loafers – again slip-ons – which had a completely pointless leather tassel on top. Loafers were supposed to look like the sort of soft deck shoe you might wear on your yacht; but if you didn't have a yacht, you just looked like you'd wandered out in your slippers.

Jackets

A jacket was more than the thing surrounding a potato to a smooth operator, though he did lounge around in his smoking jacket like a couch potato, it has to be said, whilst smoking his way through his third box of fags of the day. Smoking jackets said 'Come to bed with me'. They also made him look like he was still wearing his dressing gown. Leslie Phillips, eat your heart out: to the right is actor Peter Wyngarde, the smoothest of the smooth, sporting a smoking jacket tribute to 'Ra Ra Rasputin, Lover of the Russian Queen'. And his hair is the worst!

After all this bon-viveur campery, jackets went manly from the late '70s onwards. The denim jacket, for example, gave the smooth operator the feel of the Marlboro Man, sucking on his last fag of the day before driving the cattle back to the ranch. And what a cowboy a smooth operator was. You just wouldn't want him rewiring your electrics of repointing your brickwork, that's all. Smooth operators liked jackets that made them seem more active than they actually were – so for bomber jackets think of Douglas Bader or someone out of *Top Gun*. Leather and denim: it made the smooth operator look dead hard and butch, It also made him look like a gay hustler from the meat-packing district.

And then there was the sheepskin jacket, which was basically one of those sheepskin rugs from in front of the hearth turned inside out with buttons on. But when the smooth operator got one on his back, it was synonymous with the sort of dodgy operator who flogged videos out of the back of a Mazda.

Nightwear

There were only two forms of smooth-operator nightwear. The first was the karate black satin dressing gown, the type usually to be found with a Chinese dragon motif on the back. This look involved the wearing of skimpy tanga briefs, the spraying of Spanish fly on genitals and smoking in bed. This combination often proved to be pure ladykiller: one flick of his fag ash and both woman and nylon leopard print bedspread went up like a bush fire.

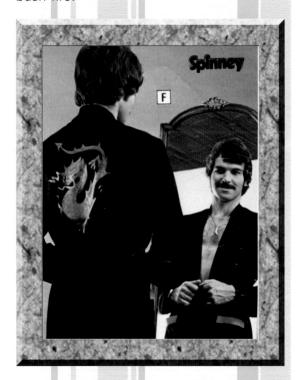

The other night attire was more catalogue-bought polyester jim-jams in regulation pink, baby blue, dusky peach or paisley variations. A smooth operator didn't scratch his arse or have his first fag of the day in these pyjamas. These were a more vivacious classification of nightwear and were often worn in the execution of activities such as pouring percolated coffee or handing around a basket of toast.

The downside of these pyjamas was that they had no fly on the front – more of a flap really – and whilst this helped the circulation, it often meant the smooth operator's cock kept falling out. Many a suburban housewife was treated to the spectacle each morning of watching the neighbourhood smooth operator getting in the gold-top with his knackers hanging out.

NIGHTWEAR

Neither look was complete without the fluffy-yet-rough dressing gowns that were cut to a risqué mid-thigh length and came in statutory stripes or checks. They wouldn't look out of place on a Girl Guides' picnic blanket or a car seat cover for a Ford Cortina. These two smoothies are enjoying the sand dunes in a way only a real man can appreciate. Both were later arrested.

Further Information

Peter Wyngarde, undoubtably the smoothest of smooth operators, was voted the sexiest man alive and was a household name because of his alter ego, playboy Jason King in the TV show *Department S*. In 1975, he was convicted of gross indecency with a truck driver in the toilets of Gloucester Bus Station, and the nation was cruelly robbed of a true superstar. We are unworthy, Peter.

For more information about the equally smooth author visit his web site at www.richardjarman.com. Richard Jarman is the author of *No Place Like Home* and *The Worst Fashion Trends in the World!*, both of which are also published by New Holland.

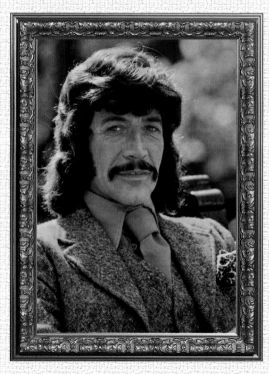

Author Acknowledgements

I would like to thank my father and his man-clogs and fuzzy perm for the inspiration for this book.

Picture Acknowledgements

All pictures courtesy of the Advertising Archives, except for p51: Rex Features 2005 and p71 (right): Arnold Diamond.

First published in 2006 by New Holland Publishers (UK) Ltd
London • Cape Town • Sydney • Auckland

10 9 8 7 6 5 4 3 2 1

www.newhollandpublishers.com

Garfield House, 86–88 Edgware Road, London W2 2EA, UK

80 McKenzie Street, Cape Town 8001, South Africa

14 Aquatic Drive, Frenchs Forest, NSW 2086, Australia

218 Lake Road, Northcote, Auckland, New Zealand

ISBN 10: 1 84537 253 0
ISBN 13: 978 1 84537 253 8

Publishing Manager: Jo Hemmings
Project Editor: Kate Parker
Cover Design and Design: Adam Morris
Production: Joan Woodroffe

Reproduction by Modern Age Repro House Ltd, Hong Kong
Printed and bound by Craft Print Pte Ltd, Singapore